the circle book

ISBN: 978-0-9860040-4-9

Distributed by:
Small Press Distribution
www.spdbooks.org

Published by:
Cuneiform Press
www.cuneiformpress.com

This book was made possible, in part, through the generous
support of UHV and friends of Cuneiform Press.

the circle book

Sommer Browning

cuneiform

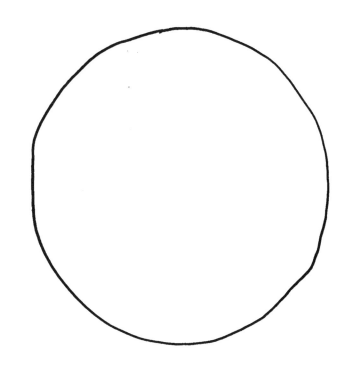

atom

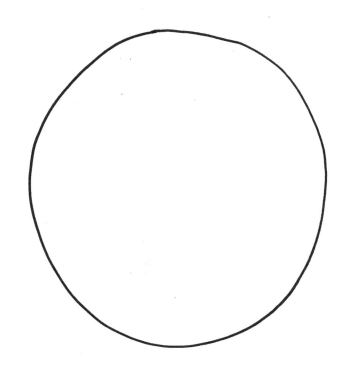

M & M

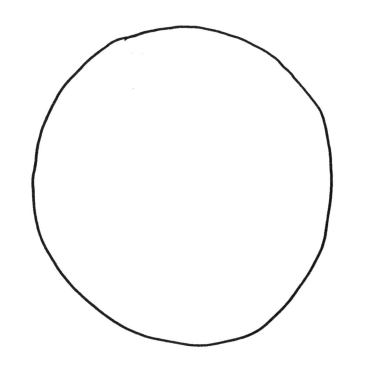

hamburger

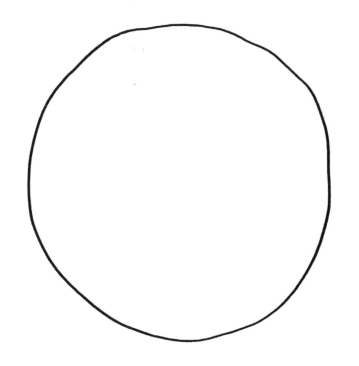

manhole cover

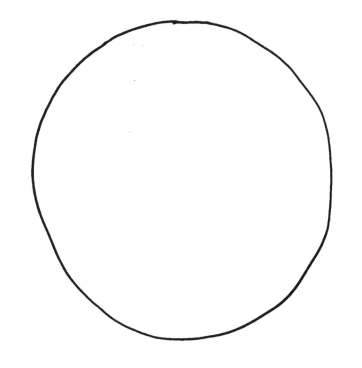

15th letter of
alphabet

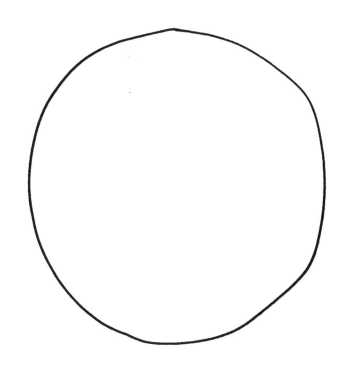

pole,
top of

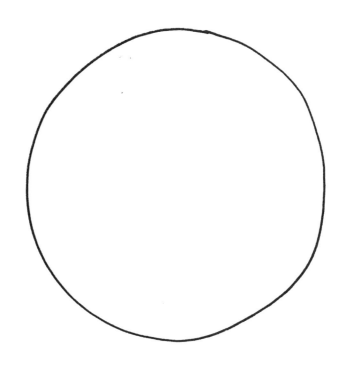

button

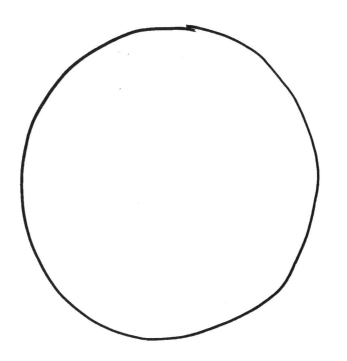

top of marshmallow

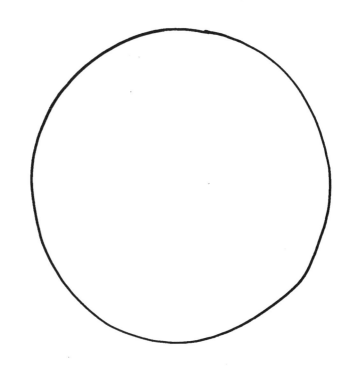

earring

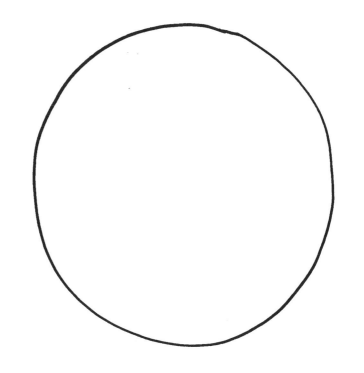

good eater

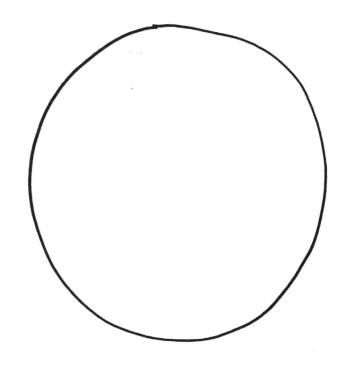

urethra

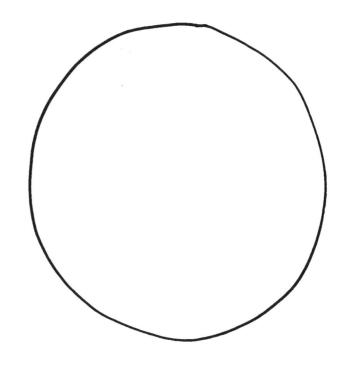

nostril

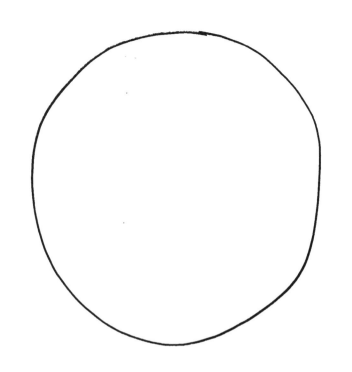

view of head from
second story walk-up

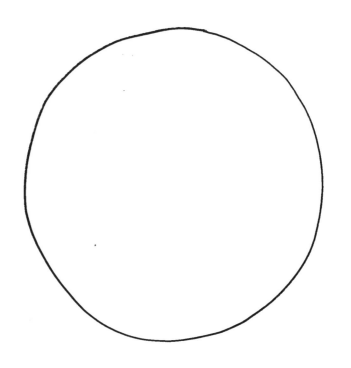

pizza

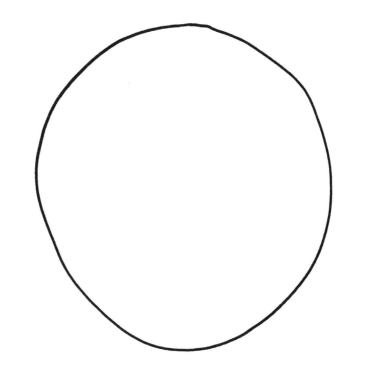

abyss

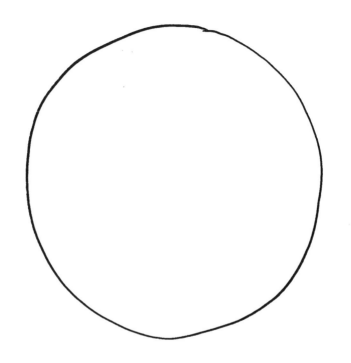

body of christ

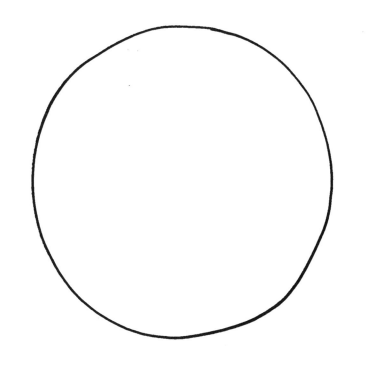

hug

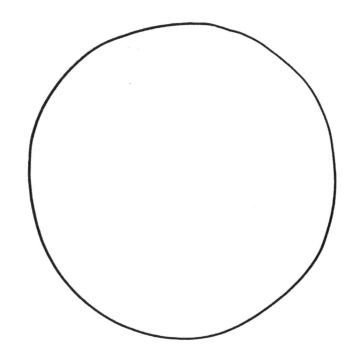

Sound hole

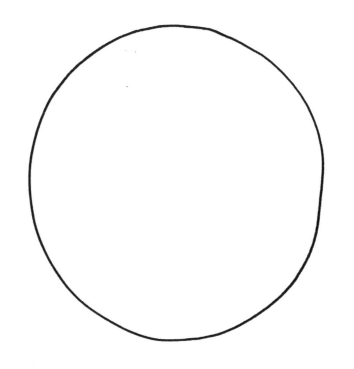

platelet

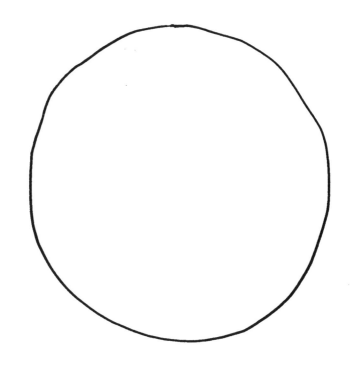

peephole

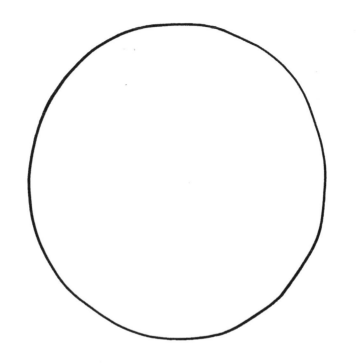

uroboros

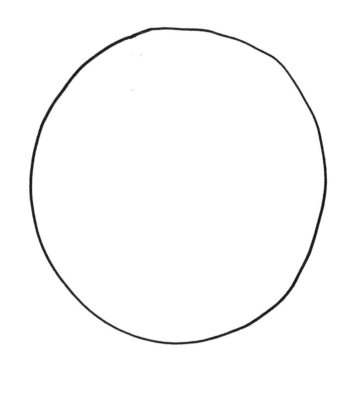

tack

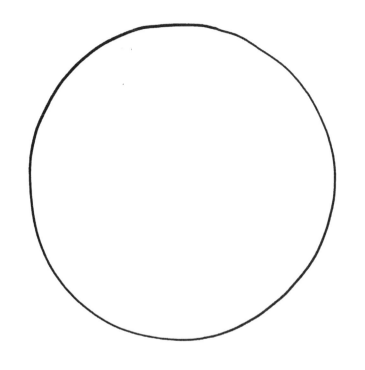

inner tube

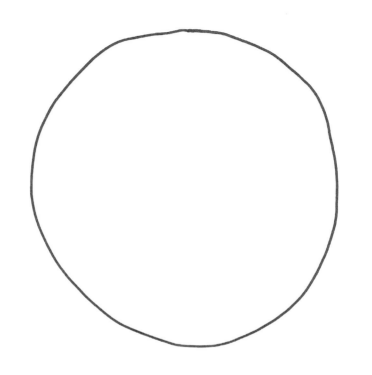

COCCUS

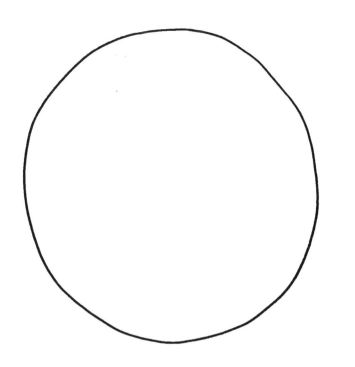

constituent component

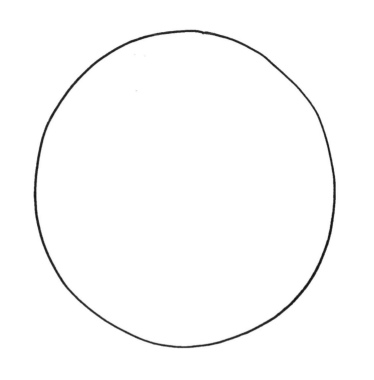

patella

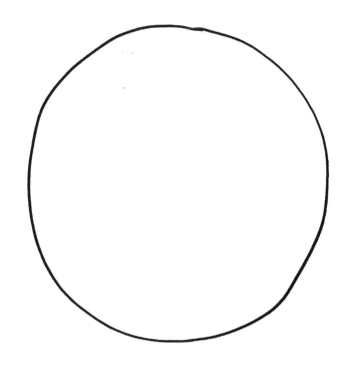

paella

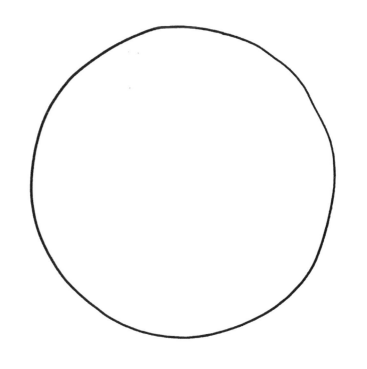

set

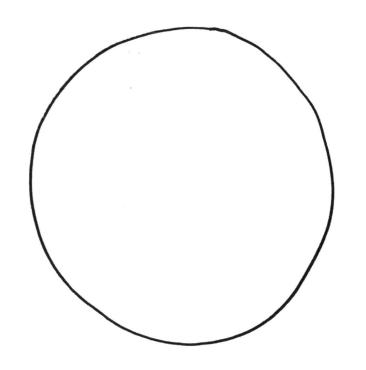

bead

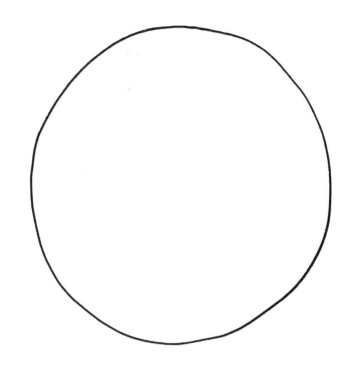

ball bearing

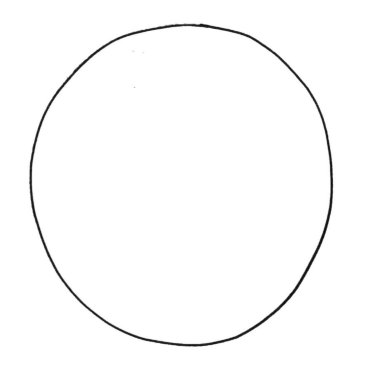

seed

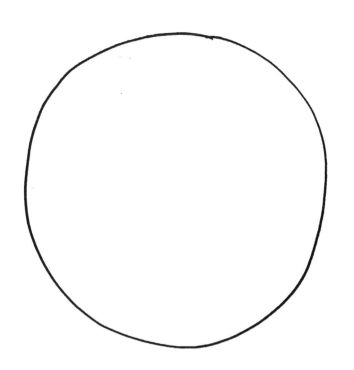

beginning of
Whitman poem

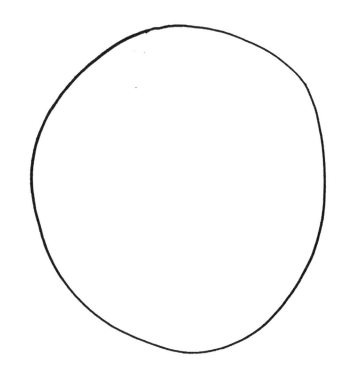

cigarette
(front view)

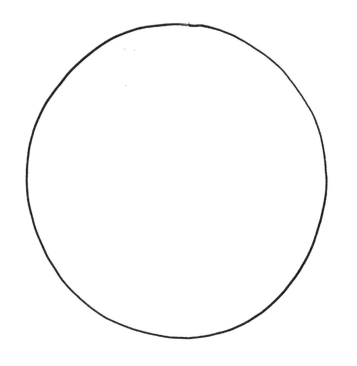

wheel

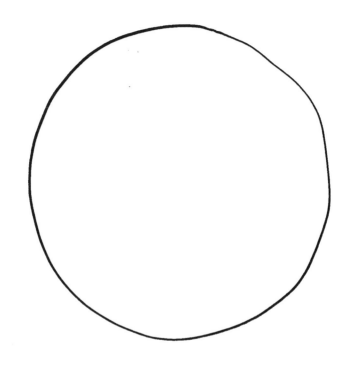

superball

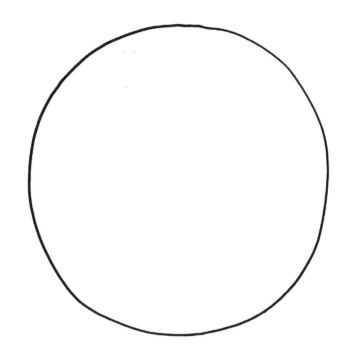

keyring

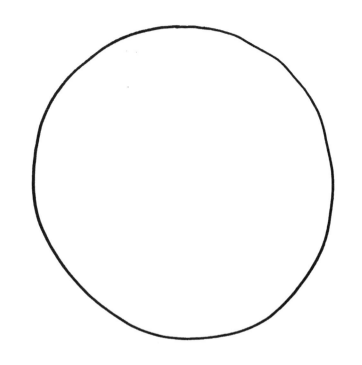

not enough

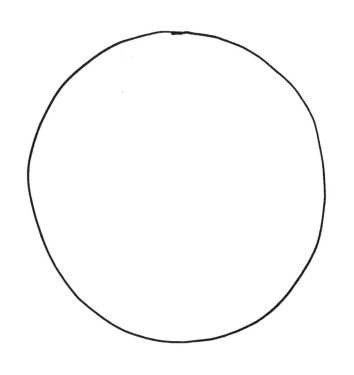

too much

pencil point
(up close)

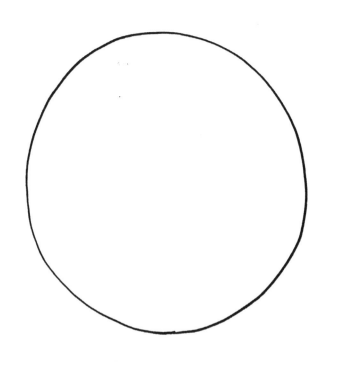

Cock and balls,
minus one cock and one ball

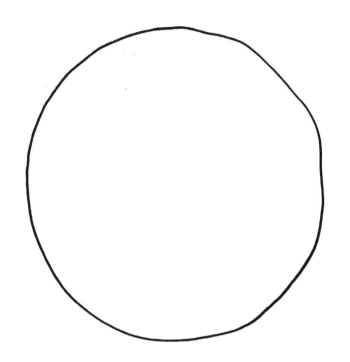

single fanged

vampire wound

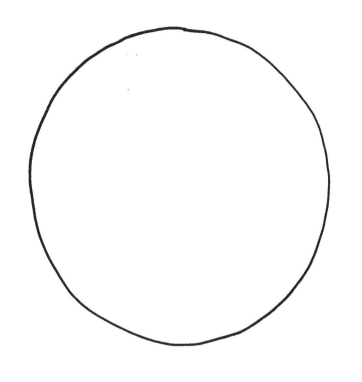

coin

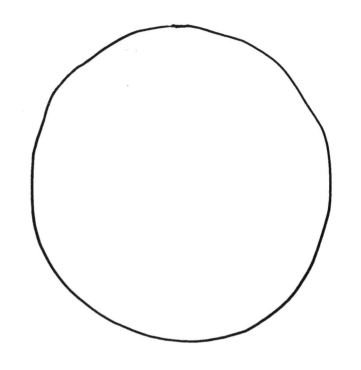

peephole

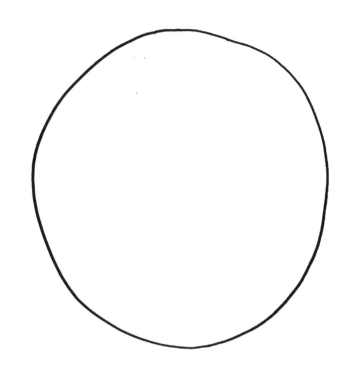

bubble

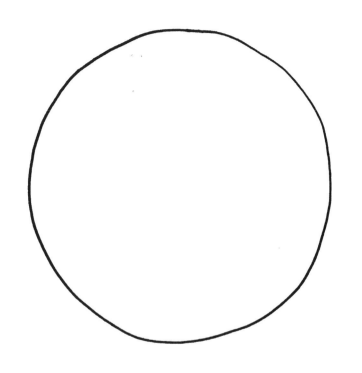

exclamation

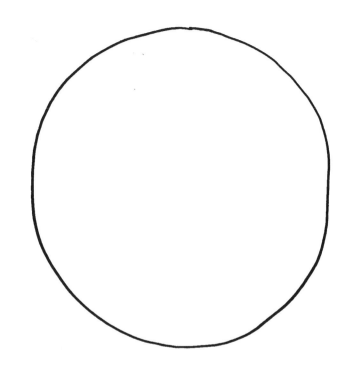

onion

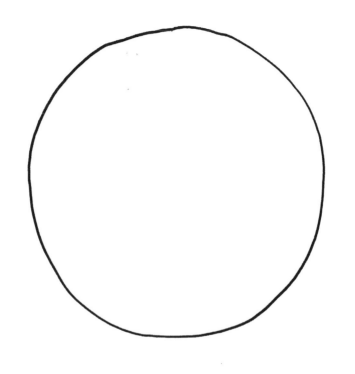

fisheye

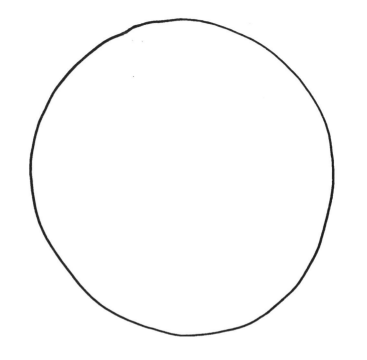

pogostick
footprint

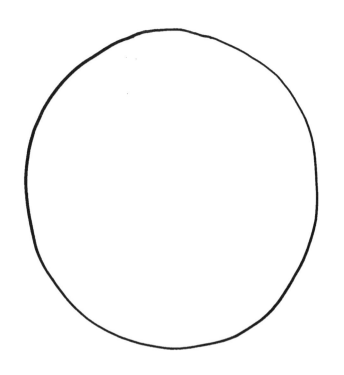

ping pong ball

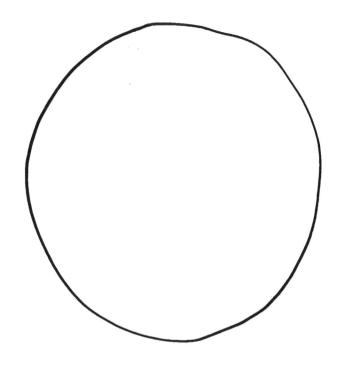

rubber band

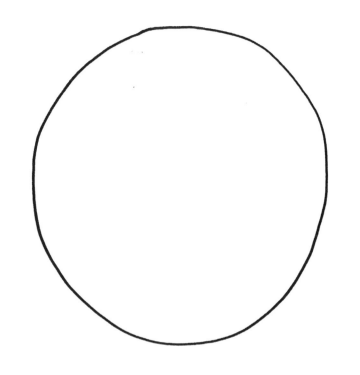

everything/
nothing

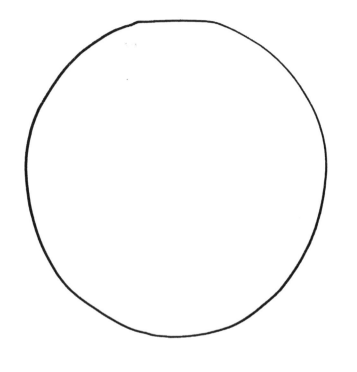

bottle cap

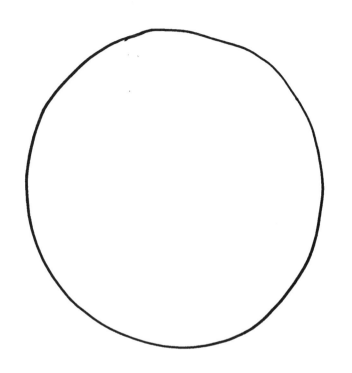

blueberry

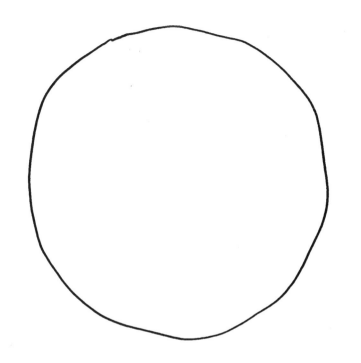

monocle

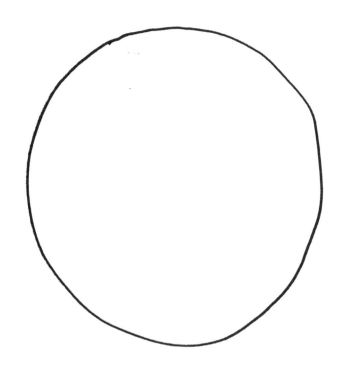

coaster

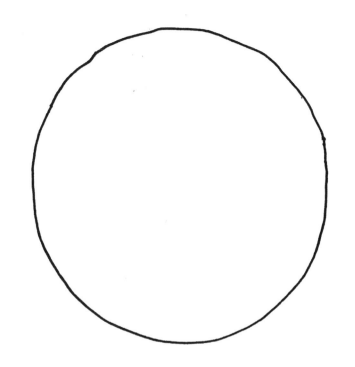

view of blizzard
through telescope

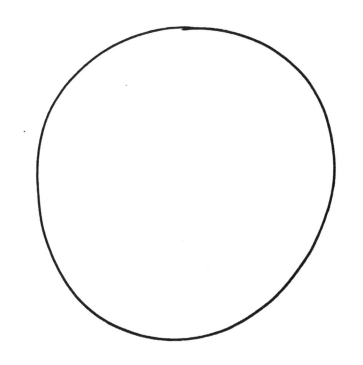

Bon Jovi's 11th
Studio album

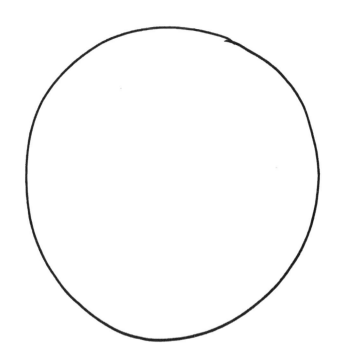

hole punch hole

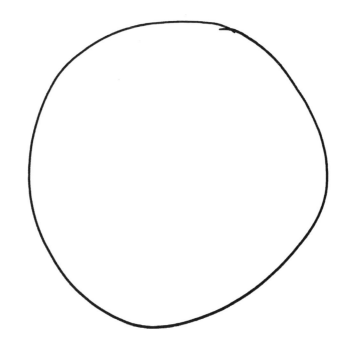

sphincter

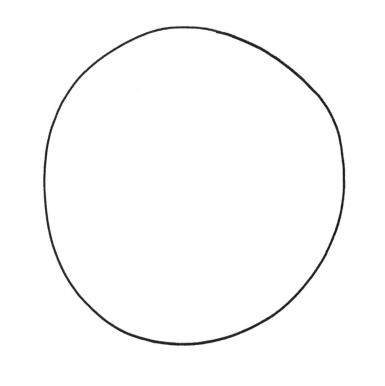

zilch

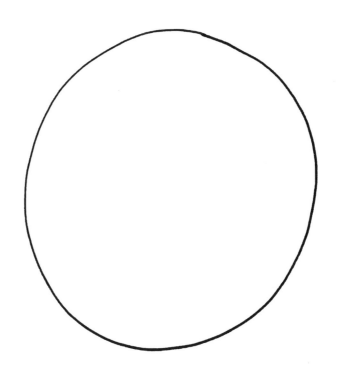

pancake

·

pencil point
(actual size)

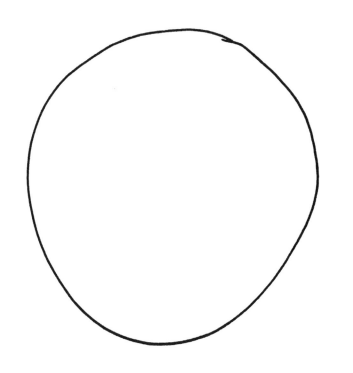

boring kaleidoscope

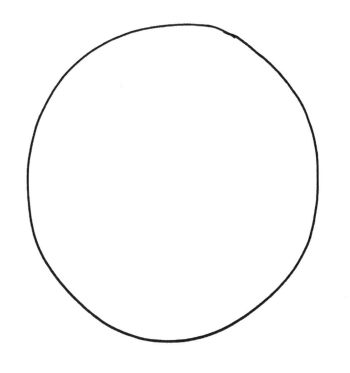

freezing

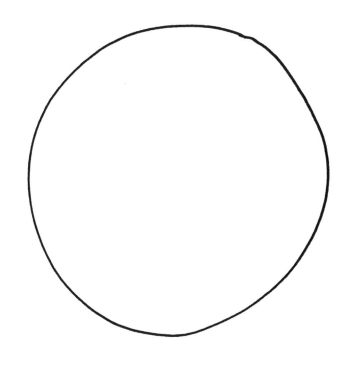

vowel

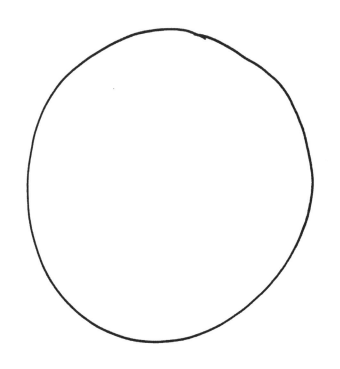

tube sock from
above

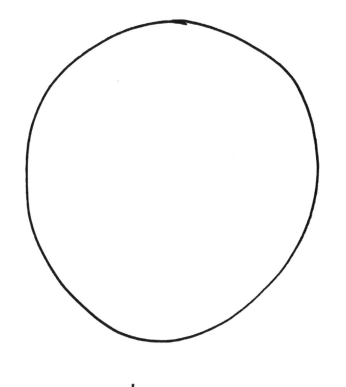

door
Knob

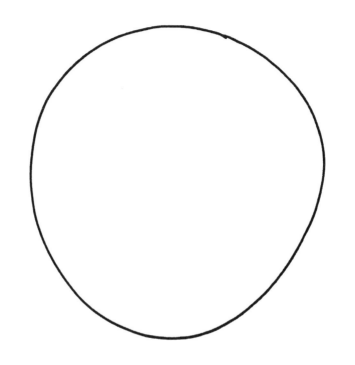

Suction cup

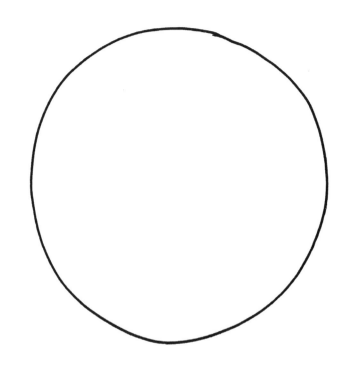

hula hoop

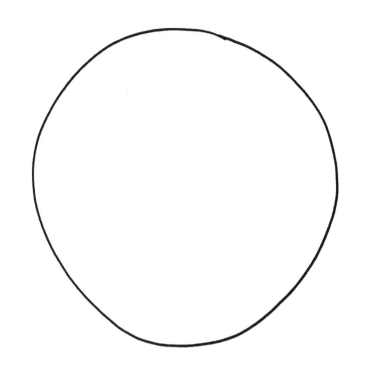

symbol

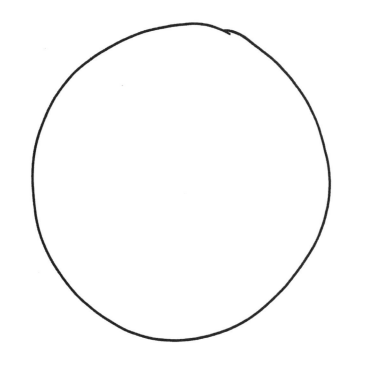

pixel

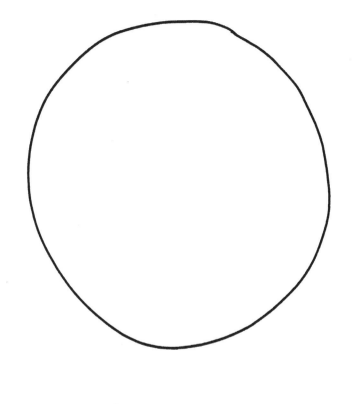

dollop

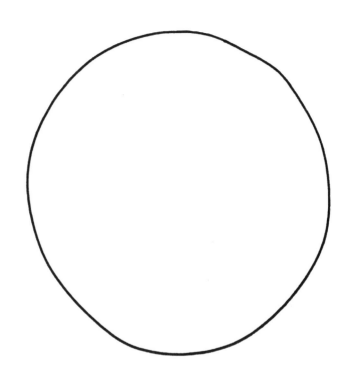

entrance wound

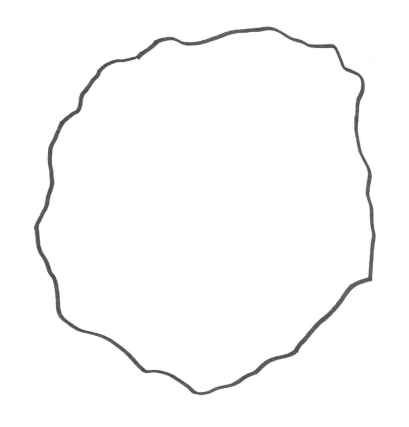

exit wound

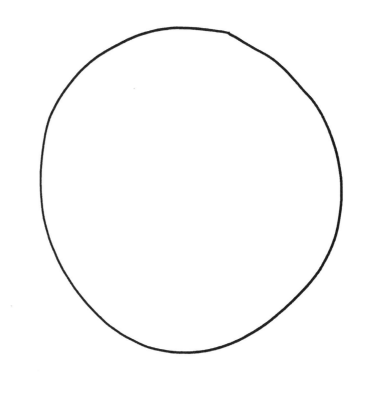

Shape

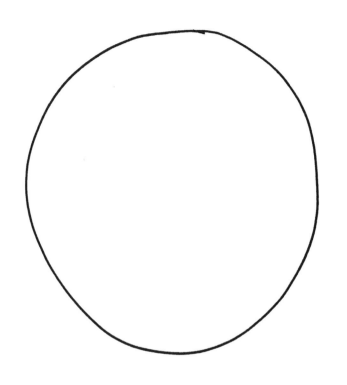

the light

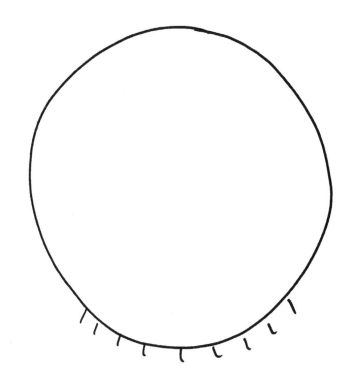

blinking cyclopes

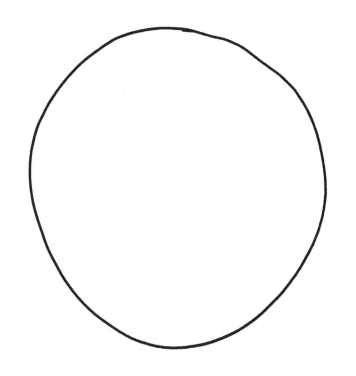

roundabout

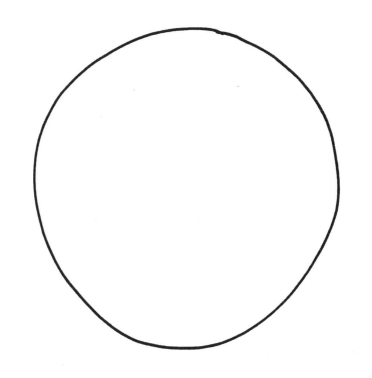

rotary

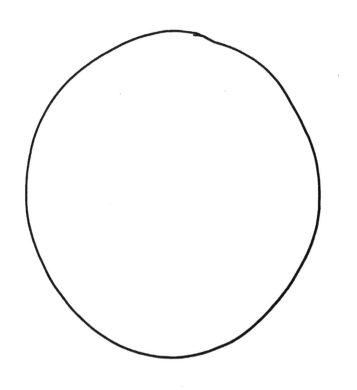

terrible score

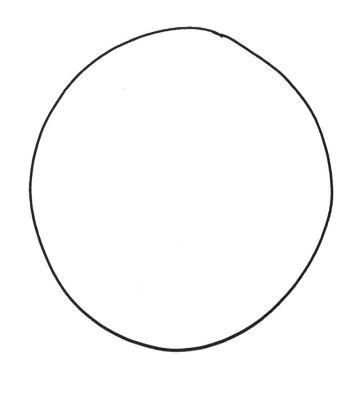

orbit

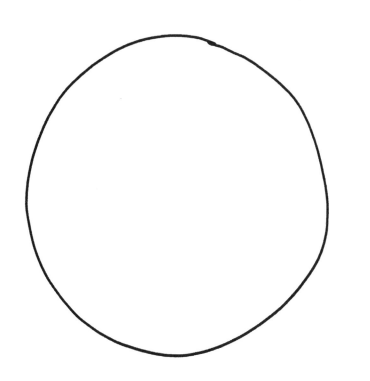

drop of tomato soup

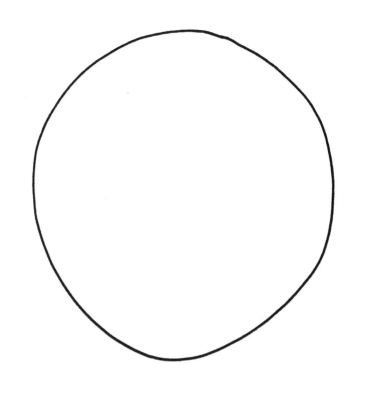

Hobbit
doorway

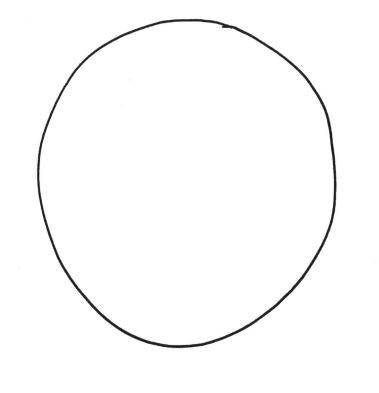

roe

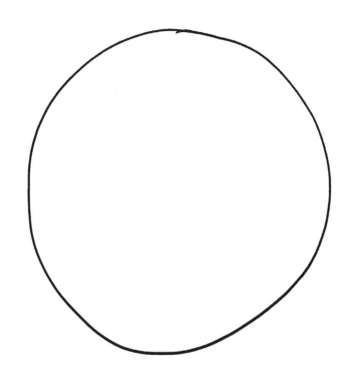

this / not this

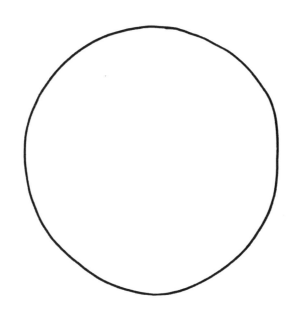

neither wavy lines,
nor cross, nor star, nor square

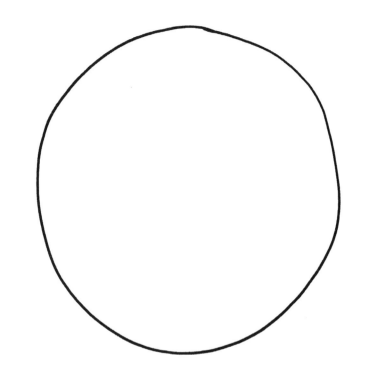

zygote

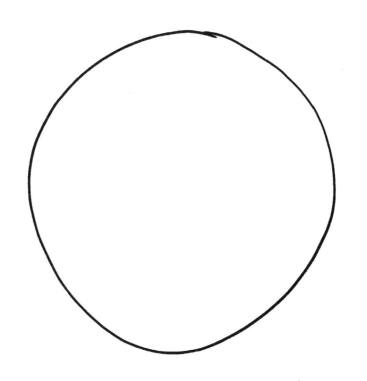

drum head

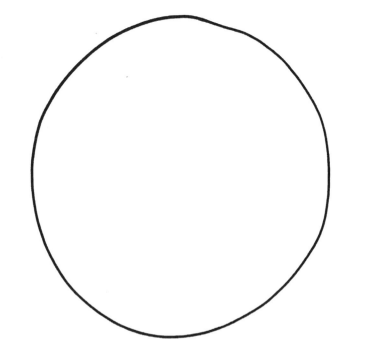

tennis ball can
traveling straight toward
you

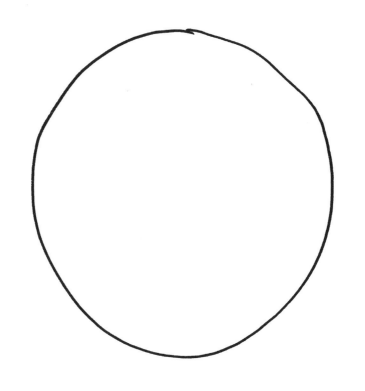

poker chip

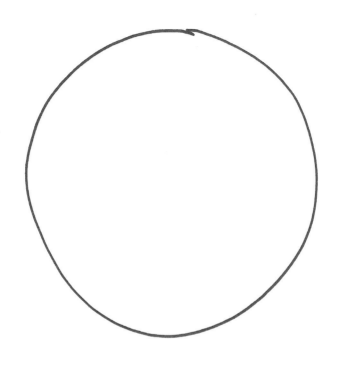

contents
of savings account

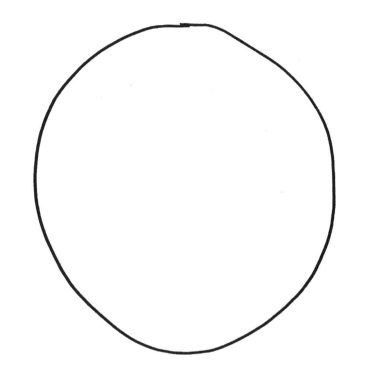

earth

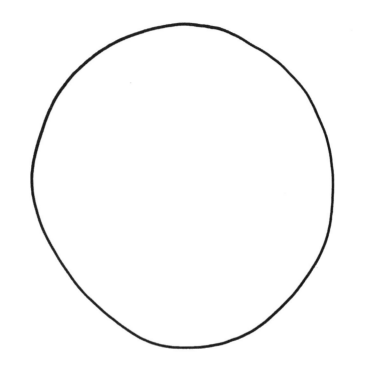

sun

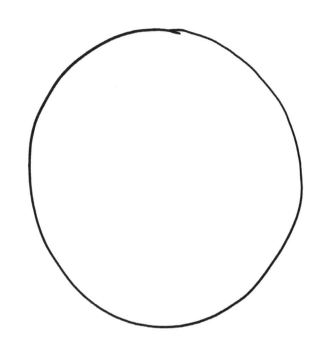

Set of points
in a plane that are a given
distance from a given
point

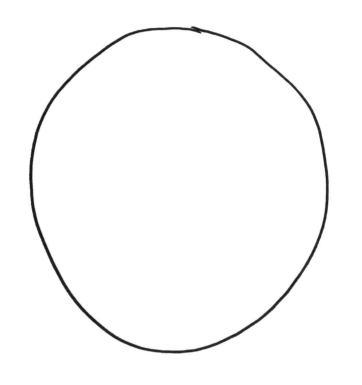

nipple

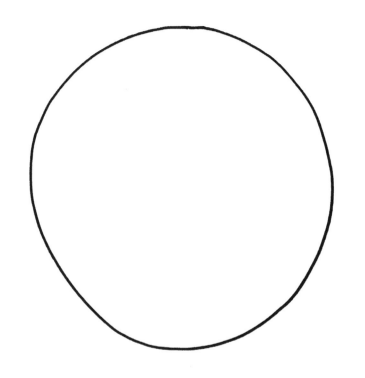

bagel hole

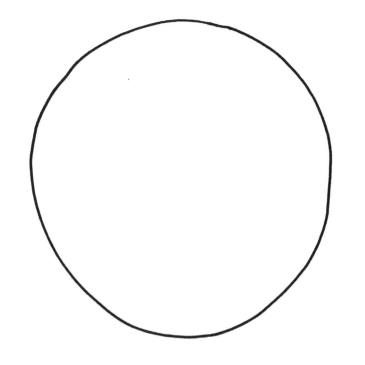

the shape of

Cameron Diaz's
face

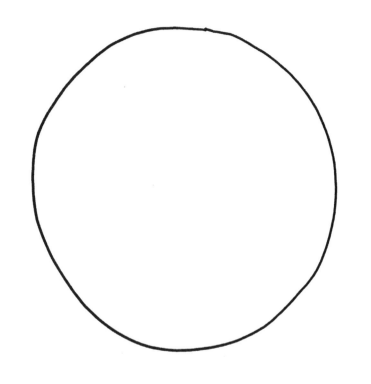

pupil

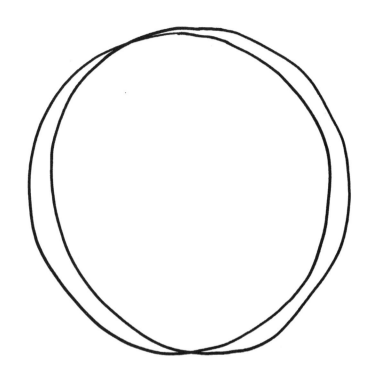

drunk

Sommer Browning writes poems, draws comics, and tells jokes in Denver. <u>Backup Singers</u> is her latest book of poetry out with Birds, LLC. She is a librarian.